Through the Looking-Glass

A classic story by Lewis Carroll
Adapted by Gill Munton

Contents

1	Through the Looking-glass	2
2	The Red Queen	11
3	Looking-glass animals	19
4	Tweedledum and Tweedledee	28
5	A sheep in a shop	36
6	Humpty Dumpty	45
7	The Lion and the Unicorn	52
8	The White Knight	61
9	Queen Alice	69
10	Alice's party	75
	Left or right?	83
	Chess	84
	About the author	88

CHAPTER 1

Through the Looking-glass

It was a cold winter day and Alice was sitting by the fire. She was rolling some wool into a ball for her mother to knit into a jumper. Soon she started to feel sleepy, so she put the ball of wool on the floor …

When Alice woke up, her cat Dinah was washing one of her kittens. It was Snowdrop (the good kitten). Alice watched as Dinah washed Snowdrop's white face.

'Poor Snowdrop,' she thought. 'I don't think she likes that. Now, where's Kitty?' Kitty was the black kitten (the naughty one).

Then Alice saw the wool. Kitty had been playing with it while Alice was asleep. Now it lay in a mess on the floor. Kitty was tangled in the wool and she was running in circles, chasing her tail.

'You naughty little cat!' cried Alice. She picked the kitten up and kissed her. (It was hard to be angry with a kitten.) She frowned at Dinah, the kittens' mother. 'You must teach her to be good, Dinah,' she said. She climbed back into her chair, taking Kitty and the wool with her.

Alice started to roll the wool up again. As she worked, she talked to the kitten, who sat next to her and watched.

'You've done three naughty things today, Kitty. First, you squeaked when Dinah was washing your face. What did you say – her paw went into your eye? Well, you must close your eyes when your mother washes your face. Then, you drank Snowdrop's milk. I know you were thirsty, but Snowdrop was thirsty, too. After that, you tangled my wool! When I saw it, Kitty, I almost cried.'

'Kitty, can you play chess?' Alice asked. 'When I was playing it with my sister, I'm sure you were watching us. I've got an idea! Let's pretend that you're the Red Queen! She's a very important chess piece.'

Alice stood up and went to the chess set on the table. She picked up the Red Queen and put her in front of the kitten.

'There, you see?' said Alice. 'Can you fold your arms like the Red Queen? You'll look just like her.'

But the kitten did not fold her arms. She started to play with the wool again.

'You naughty kitten!' Alice said. She picked her up and climbed onto the shelf above the fire. She held Kitty up so that the kitten could see herself in the looking-glass. (This was the big mirror above the fire.)

'Look at your naughty face!' said Alice. 'To punish you, I think I'll put you into the Looking-glass House. How would you like that, Kitty? Now listen – I'll tell you about the Looking-glass House. The room you can see is the same as this room – but everything is back to front.

'I can see the chair and the table and the books. They're like our books, but the words go the wrong way. I wish I could see the fireplace. Do you think they have a fire?

'Would you like to live in the Looking-glass House, Kitty? Do you think they would give you milk? Oh, I wish I could go through the Looking-glass! Let's pretend that the glass is soft – oh, Kitty, I think it's melting! Like ice!'

'The glass is melting into a silver mist ...' thought Alice. '... I've gone through the Looking-glass! I'm in the Looking-glass House!'

Alice jumped down. First, she looked in the fireplace. 'Good! There's a fire here, too. I won't be cold,' she thought.

Then she looked at the pictures on the walls. Everything in them was moving and the clock had a face! It looked like an old man and he was smiling at Alice.

Alice looked down at the floor. 'What an untidy room,' she said. 'All the chess pieces are on the floor! There are pieces of coal, too, from the fireplace.'

Alice knelt down to look at the chess pieces. 'They're walking about!' she whispered. (She did not want to frighten them.) 'I can see the Red Queen and the Red King … and there are the White Queen and the White King … and the two White Castles. I don't think they can hear me or see me, though. Perhaps I'm invisible.'

Then Alice heard a little squeak. 'It's coming from the table,' she thought. She stood up and went to look. One of the White Pawns was rolling about on the table. She was kicking her legs in the air and squeaking.

'It's my little daughter, Lily!' cried the White Queen. 'I must go to her!' She pushed past the White King, who fell among the pieces of coal. 'I'm coming, my dear!' she cried, trying to climb up one of the table legs.

'What a fuss,' said the White King angrily. He was covered in coal dust and he had hurt his nose.

Poor little Lily was screaming now, so Alice picked up the White Queen and put her on the table. The White Queen hugged her daughter until she was quiet and then she called out to the White King, 'Be careful with the tornado, my dear!'

'What tornado?' he replied. 'Where is it?' He looked in the fireplace. 'Is it in here?'

'The tornado that blew me up onto the table, silly,' replied the White Queen. 'If you want to join us, you can climb up.'

The White King tried to climb up the table leg, but he was very slow.

'Poor thing,' thought Alice. She picked him up and gently brushed off the coal dust with her hand. He was so surprised that his eyes and his mouth grew bigger and bigger, and rounder and rounder. Alice laughed so much that she almost dropped him.

She put the White King on the table with the White Queen and Lily. 'He looks quite ill,' she said to herself. 'I'll find some water to splash on his face.' When she got back to the table with the water, the White King looked much better. He was talking to the White Queen and Alice knelt down to listen.

'I was so frightened, my dear,' the White King said. 'I'll never forget it.'

'You *will* forget it,' the White Queen replied, 'if you don't write it all in your notebook.'

So the White King took his notebook from his pocket and started to write.

As Alice waited for the White King to finish writing, she saw a pile of books on the table. She picked one up, opened it and saw a poem. But when she tried to read it, she could not understand the words. 'This poem is very strange,' she said to herself. 'I don't think it's written in English.' This is what she saw:

'Twas brillig, and the slithy toves
Did gyre and gimble in the wabe.
All mimsy were the borogoves,
And the mome raths outgrabe.

Alice looked at the poem for a long time. Then she had an idea. 'It's a Looking-glass book!' she said to herself. 'So it's a Looking-glass poem! All the words are back to front. If I put the poem in front of the Looking-glass, I can read it.'

So she climbed up onto the shelf again and held the book up. In the Looking-glass, she read:

'Twas brillig, and the slithy toves
Did gyre and gimble in the wabe.
All mimsy were the borogoves,
And the mome raths outgrabe.

'But I still don't understand it,' said poor Alice. 'It's a nonsense poem.' Then she remembered where she was and she jumped up. 'I won't stay here any longer,' she said to herself. 'I want to see the rest of the Looking-glass House. I'll go outside and look at the garden.'

So she ran out of the room and went to the top of the stairs. She put her foot on the first step and suddenly she was flying down to the bottom! She flew along the hall, out of the door and into the garden.

CHAPTER 2

The Red Queen

'It's a beautiful garden,' Alice said to herself, 'and I can see a hill. If I climb to the top of it, I'll be able to see everything. I'll walk along this path – I think it will take me to the bottom of the hill.'

She started walking, but there were lots of twists and turns in the path. Soon she was back at the Looking-glass House. She tried a different path, but the same thing happened.

'I don't want to go back into the Looking-glass House yet,' she said. 'I want to have lots of adventures first. I'll try to find the hill again.'

The third path went to a large flowerbed. Alice could see tiger lilies, daisies and lots of pink roses. 'What pretty flowers!' she said to herself. She looked at one of the tiger lilies waving about in the wind. 'I wish you could talk,' she said. 'I don't like talking to myself.' She was very surprised when the flower replied!

'We *can* talk,' said the Tiger Lily. 'But we only speak to important people. Are you important?'

'Oh! I must be!' whispered Alice. 'Can all the flowers here talk?'

'Oh, yes,' said the Tiger Lily. 'We can all speak English as well as you can. It's really not difficult, you know.'

Then one of the roses joined in. 'We were waiting for you to speak first,' she said. Then she went on, 'I like your face. It's pink, like mine.'

'I don't care about the colour,' said the Tiger Lily, 'but I don't like your petals – they're much too straight. Curly petals are best. As you can see, *I* have curly petals.'

All the little daisies started shouting. 'No! Nonsense! Straight petals are best.'

They made so much noise that the Tiger Lily shook with anger. 'If I could reach you, you wouldn't dare to be so naughty!' she told them.

Alice bent down and whispered to the daisies, 'If you don't stop that noise, I'll pick you!'

There was silence then and some of the pink daisies were so frightened that their petals turned white.

'That's better,' said the Tiger Lily. 'They all speak together and I don't like it.'

'Tell me this,' said Alice. 'I've been in lots of gardens and the flowers couldn't talk. But you all can. Why?'

'Put your hand down and feel the earth in the flowerbed,' said the Tiger Lily.

Alice did.

'It's very hard, isn't it?' the Tiger Lily continued. 'And you can't sleep in a hard bed, can you? Well, most flowers grow in *soft* earth, so they're always asleep. And you can't talk if you're asleep.'

'Oh, yes,' said Alice. 'I didn't think of that.'

'You don't think at all!' replied the Rose.

'That's true!' said a tiny violet.

'Be quiet, Violet!' cried the Tiger Lily. 'You hide under the leaves all day. You don't know anything!'

Alice decided to ask another question. 'Am I the only person in this garden?' she said.

'People are just flowers who can walk,' replied the Rose. 'I wish I could walk – I really don't know how you do it. There's another one like you, but she has a thicker stalk.'

'Perhaps there's another little girl in the garden!' thought Alice. 'I'd like that – we could play together.'

'Does she look like me?' she asked. 'Has she got long blonde hair and blue eyes?'

'She's the same shape as you,' said the Rose, 'but she's red and her petals are much shorter.'

'Yes, and they're tidy,' added the Tiger Lily. 'Your petals are very untidy.'

'And she has spikes round her head,' said the Rose. 'You'll meet her soon. She often walks in the garden.'

Alice sighed. 'She's not like me at all,' she thought.

'I think she's coming now!' cried the Tiger Lily, waving her petals. 'I can hear her footsteps on the path. Thump, thump, thump!'

Alice turned round and smiled. 'I know who that is! It's the Red Queen!' she said to herself. 'But she's much bigger now.

She's bigger than I am! I think I'll go to meet her. I like talking to flowers, but now I can talk to a real Queen. That's much more exciting.'

'Oh, you can't go to meet her,' said the Rose. 'You must walk away from her if you want to talk to her.'

Alice thought this was nonsense and so she started to walk towards the Red Queen. But soon the Red Queen disappeared and Alice was back at the Looking-glass House. She walked round the garden, looking for the Red Queen. At last she saw her, but she was far away.

'I'll do what the Rose said,' Alice thought. She started to walk away from the Red Queen. Very soon, she was standing next to her.

'Good afternoon,' said Alice.

'Who are you and where are you going?' the Red Queen wanted to know. 'Look up, speak nicely and keep your hands still.'

'My name's Alice. I was walking in the garden, but I – I've lost my path,' Alice replied.

'Lost your path? Lost your path? It isn't your path, you know. All the paths are mine!' cried the Red Queen. 'But why are you here in the garden?'

'I was in the Looking-glass House and I wanted to see the garden, Your Majesty,' Alice replied politely. 'If I can get to the top of that hill, I'll be able to see it all.'

'All right,' said the Red Queen more kindly. 'Come with me. I'll show you the way to the hill.'

The Red Queen led Alice to the bottom of the hill and they climbed to the top. Alice could see the garden and the countryside around it.

'It looks very strange,' she said. 'There are lots of squares with streams and hedges between them. It's just like a giant chessboard! Perhaps someone is playing a giant game of chess! I wish I could be one of the pieces. I could be a Pawn. Each player has eight Pawns and they're the smallest pieces. But I'd really love to be a Queen, of course.'

Alice looked up at the Red Queen, afraid that she would be angry now. But the Red Queen smiled and said, 'You can be in the chess game if you like. Now let me think – I know! You can start as one of the White Pawns because little Lily is too young to play. When you get to the eighth square, you can be a Queen.'

Alice felt very excited by this. Could she really be a Queen? But suddenly the Red Queen took her hand and cried, 'Come on! We must run now!'

And then they were running, faster and faster and faster!

'We never pass anything,' thought Alice. 'It's very strange. We're running as fast as the wind, but all the trees and plants stay in the same place. Are they moving with us?'

But the Red Queen just said, 'Faster! We must go faster!'

'Are we nearly there?' asked Alice. She didn't think she could run any more.

'Oh, yes, we're nearly there!' replied the Red Queen. 'We arrived ten minutes ago. Run faster, run faster!'

Now they were going so fast that their feet left the ground. They were flying! The wind whistled in Alice's ears and almost blew her hair off her head.

At last they stopped. Alice felt dizzy and the Red Queen said, 'You can rest now. Lean against this tree.'

As she rested, Alice looked up at the tree. 'This is where we started!' she said in surprise. 'We were in the same place all the time!'

'That's right,' said the Red Queen.

'But in *my* country,' said poor Alice, 'if you run very fast for a long time, you get to a different place.'

'Here,' said the Red Queen, 'we have to run just to stand still. If we want to go somewhere else, we run even faster! Shall we try that?'

'Oh, no, I'm happy to stay here,' said Alice quickly. She didn't want to run any more. 'But I *am* so hot and thirsty after all that running.'

'Perhaps she'll give me something to drink,' Alice hoped.

But the Red Queen took a little box from her pocket and said, 'Would you like a biscuit?'

Alice took one politely. 'I wish it was a glass of water,' she thought. 'But this *is* Looking-glass Land. Everything is upside down and back to front.'

Then the Red Queen asked Alice, 'Would you like another biscuit?'

'No, thank you, Your Majesty,' Alice said quickly. The last biscuit she ate was very dry and she did not want to eat another one.

'Good. So you aren't thirsty any more,' replied the Red Queen.

Alice did not know what to say to this, so she said nothing.

'Now,' said the Red Queen, 'I'll tell you what you must do. You're a Pawn and Pawns can move forward two squares when they start the game. You're in the second square now and you'll go through the third square very quickly – by train, I think.

'At the edge of the third square, there's a little stream. In the fourth square, you'll find Tweedledum and Tweedledee in a forest. They're twins, you know. I think you'll like them. The fifth square is mostly water and the sixth square belongs to Humpty Dumpty. The seventh square is another forest – but one of the Knights will show you the way through it. In the eighth square, we'll be Queens together. The White Queen will be there, too, and we'll have a party! What fun we'll have!'

And then she was gone.

'Perhaps she ran into the forest,' thought Alice. 'I know she can run very fast. Well, I'm ready to start the game of chess now.'

CHAPTER 3

Looking-glass animals

From the top of the hill, Alice looked down at the giant chessboard. Far away, she could see an animal flying round a flower.

'I don't think it's a bee,' she said to herself. 'It's much bigger than a bee. Oh, it's an elephant! Those flowers must be as big as houses. Houses with stalks! The elephants must make lots of honey! I think I'll go down and watch them ... No, perhaps I won't. They may be dangerous. I'll go down the hill and into the third square. I want to get to the fourth square soon to meet Tweedledum and Tweedledee.'

So Alice ran down the hill.

Alice was soon in the third square. She was sitting on a train with a Goat, a Beetle and a Horse. A man dressed in white clothes was sitting opposite Alice. He was reading a newspaper.

'I'm on a train now! That's very strange. I wonder where we're going,' she thought.

The ticket collector stood on the platform. He was looking through the window of the train. 'Tickets, please!' he cried. 'Show me your train tickets, ladies and gentlemen!'

All the other passengers showed him their tickets and then he looked at Alice. 'Show me your ticket, child!' he said angrily.

Everyone else joined in. 'Hurry!' they said. 'You must show him your ticket!'

'I'm very sorry, but I don't have a ticket,' said Alice. 'I didn't see a ticket office, so I couldn't buy one.'

'Don't make excuses. You should have bought one from the driver,' replied the ticket collector. Then he took a pair of binoculars from his pocket and looked at Alice.

After a minute, he frowned at her and said, 'You're going the wrong way.' He shut the window and walked away.

'You should know which way you're going,' said the man in white, looking up from his newspaper.

'You should also know where the ticket office is,' added the Goat. He shut his eyes and went to sleep.

'When you go back,' said the Beetle, 'you'll have to pretend you're a parcel because you don't have a ticket. Parcels don't need tickets.'

'They'll have to stick a label on you,' laughed the Horse. 'It will say: Little girl – please do not drop!'

There were lots more ideas. Each idea was sillier than the one before.

'She could pretend to be a letter. Then she could be posted.'

'She could pull the train! Then she wouldn't need a ticket.'

Alice was angry now. 'Stop that!' she said. 'I won't be a parcel with a silly label on it! I won't be a letter and I won't pull the train! I don't know why I'm on the train at all. I'm only a Pawn in a game of chess!'

Then she heard a tiny voice: 'Will you be my friend? I'm just a little insect ...'

Alice was very surprised by this. She looked around, but she could not see an insect. 'I hope it can't sting,' she said to herself. 'I don't like insects that can sting. I wonder what type of insect it is ...'

Then the passengers heard a loud whistle from the train and everyone jumped up. The Horse opened the window and looked out.

'It's all right,' he said. 'We're coming to a little stream and the train will have to jump over it.'

'Jump over it? How can a train jump?' wondered Alice. 'But I'm pleased that we're at the stream. The Red Queen said that the stream is at the edge of the third square. So we're nearly in the fourth square.'

And then the train flew up into the air. Alice was frightened and she grabbed the nearest thing. It was the Goat's beard. Everything felt soft and fluffy, and Alice closed her eyes ...

When she opened her eyes again, Alice was sitting under a tree. The Goat's beard had disappeared and so had the Goat, the train and all the other passengers.

'I must be in the fourth square now,' she thought. 'But where are Tweedledum and Tweedledee?'

Above her head, an insect was sitting on the branch of a tree, flapping its wings. 'Hello! I'm a gnat,' he said. 'I'm the insect who whispered to you on the train. Do you like insects?'

Alice looked up at it in surprise. 'I like insects who can talk,' she replied. 'I've never met a talking insect before.'

'What are the insects in your country?' asked the Gnat.

Alice started to count them on her fingers. 'There's the Horse Fly ...'

'Well, here in Looking-glass Land, we have a Rocking Horse Fly,' said the Gnat. 'Look in that bush and you'll see one. It's made of wood and it swings from branch to branch on its rocker.'

Alice looked at the Rocking Horse Fly with great interest. It had bright, shiny red spots. 'I think it's just been painted,' she said. 'What does it eat?'

'It eats paper,' replied the Gnat. 'What other insects do you know?'

'Well, there's the Butterfly ...' Alice said.

'Aha! Remember – you're in Looking-glass Land now,' said the Gnat. 'Look down at your feet, and you'll see a Bread and Butter Fly. Its wings are thin slices of bread and butter, its body is a crust of bread and its head is a lump of sugar.'

Alice looked down and saw the Bread and Butter Fly. It had long hairy legs and it was crawling towards her. She jumped back quickly. 'What does this one eat?' she asked.

'Tea with milk in it,' the Gnat replied.

Alice thought about this. 'But there isn't any tea or milk here,' she said. 'What happens if a Bread and Butter Fly can't find any?'

'It dies, of course,' said the Gnat. 'If you don't eat and drink, you die.'

'But that must happen very often,' said Alice with a frown.

'It always happens,' replied the Gnat sadly. He flew round and round Alice's head a few times. Then he went back to his branch and said, 'I'm glad I'm called a Gnat. Over there, there's a forest. No one and nothing in that forest has a name. It must be terrible to lose your name.'

'Yes,' Alice replied.

'But on the other hand, it could be a good thing,' the Gnat went on. 'Think of your teacher. If you had no name, she couldn't call you to your lessons. Then you wouldn't have to go to them.'

'She would just call me "**Miss**",' said Alice, 'and I'd still have to go to my lessons.'

'No, you wouldn't,' laughed the Gnat. 'If she called you "Miss", you would **miss** your lessons! That's a joke, of course.'

'Well, it's a very bad joke,' replied Alice.

The Gnat sighed and two tears rolled down his cheeks.

When Alice looked up again, the Gnat had gone.

'He's disappeared,' said Alice to herself. 'I think I upset him because I didn't laugh at his joke. But I'm cold now after sitting here for so long. It's time to go.' She stood up and walked further into the fourth square.

Soon Alice came to a field with a forest on the other side. 'It's a very dark forest,' she thought. 'I don't really want to go into it. But I can't go back. This is the only way to the fifth square.' So she walked across the field. Soon she came to the forest and she went in.

'It's very cool here in the – oh, what's it called? I can't remember ...' she said to herself. 'And I'm standing under a nice leafy – I can't remember that name, either.

'Of course! Nothing has a name in here. The Gnat told me that. Perhaps I'll lose *my* name now. I'll have to get a new one. I hope it's a pretty name. But I wonder who will get my old name. How can I find out? I'll have to call everyone Alice and wait for someone to answer ...'

She thought about this for a few minutes. Then she said, 'Oh, no! It's happened! I can't remember my name! But I think it begins with "L" ...'

Suddenly, an animal jumped out from behind the trees and looked at Alice. His fur was brown with white spots.

'Hello,' she said. 'You look very friendly. You have such beautiful dark eyes.' She stretched out her hand and stroked his nose.

'What's your name?' the animal asked. His voice was soft and sweet.

'I don't know,' said poor Alice. 'I've forgotten it. Can you tell me *your* name?'

'I can't remember it *here,*' he replied. 'We must walk through the forest and out the other side. Then I'll be able to tell you my name.'

Alice put her arms round her new friend's neck and

they walked on together. But when they came to a gap in the forest, the animal jumped away from Alice and cried, 'I remember now! I'm a Fawn! I'm a baby deer. But you're a child! A human child!' And he ran away across the field as fast as he could go.

'Oh, dear. I've lost my new friend,' said Alice to herself. 'I think he's afraid of me because I'm a human. He thinks I might hurt him. But at least I can remember my name now – it's Alice, of course.'

She walked on and soon she came to a signpost. There were two signs, but they both pointed the same way. One said 'To Tweedledum's house' and the other said 'To Tweedledee's house'.

'Perhaps they live in the *same* house,' thought Alice. 'I'll go and visit them, but I won't stay for long. I'll say hello and then I'll ask them how I can get out of this forest. I want to get to the eighth square before nighttime.'

CHAPTER 4

Tweedledum and Tweedledee

Alice turned a corner and then she saw them. They were standing very still under a tree. Two little round men, exactly the same. There was only one difference. One of the men had 'DUM' on his collar and the other had 'DEE'.

'They look like schoolboys,' thought Alice.
They were standing so still that she forgot they were alive. She thought, 'I wonder if they both have "TWEEDLE" on the backs of their collars. I'll go and look.'

But as she walked up to the two little men, 'DUM' said, 'If you think we're statues, you must pay to see us. It isn't free, you know.'

Then 'DEE' added, 'But if you think we're alive, you must speak to us. You must be polite.'

'I'm sorry,' said Alice. 'I was very rude.'

Alice knew a song about Tweedledum and Tweedledee. She could hear it in her head:

Tweedledum and Tweedledee
Agreed to have a battle.
For Tweedledum said Tweedledee
Had spoiled his nice new rattle.

Just then flew down a monstrous crow,
As black as a tar barrel,
Which frightened both the heroes so,
They quite forgot their quarrel.

'When I get home, I'll tell my sister that I remembered all the words,' thought Alice. Then she said to the two little men, 'Can you help me, please? I want to find a way out of this forest.'

Tweedledum and Tweedledee looked at each other. Then Tweedledum said, 'When you visit someone, you don't start asking questions. You shake hands.'

He held out his right hand and Tweedledee held out his left hand. Alice shook their hands politely.

'Now we'll dance together,' said Tweedledum.

Still holding hands, they started to dance. Alice could hear music. 'It's coming from the tree,' she thought. 'The branches are rubbing together to make music.'

The twins were very fat and they could not dance for long. 'We've gone round four times,' gasped Tweedledee. 'That's enough for one dance.'

'What shall I say now?' wondered Alice. 'It's much too late to say hello!' So she said, 'I hope you're not very tired after the dancing.'

'No, we're not,' replied Tweedledum. 'But thank you for asking.'

Then Alice heard a strange noise. It sounded like a train – or a wild animal.

'Are there any tigers in this forest?' she asked, feeling a bit frightened.

'No. There are no tigers,' said Tweedledee. 'It's only the Red King – he's asleep and he's snoring! Let's go to see him.'

The twins led Alice to a tall tree. She could see the Red King sleeping under it. He wore a tall red nightcap with a tassel on the end and he was snoring loudly.

Alice said, 'The grass is very wet. I hope it doesn't make him ill.' (She was a kind child.)

'He's dreaming,' said Tweedledee. 'What do you think he's dreaming about?'

'I don't know,' Alice replied. 'Nobody knows that.'

'I do! He's dreaming about you!' cried Tweedledee, clapping his hands. 'And if he *stops* dreaming about you, where will you be?'

'I'll be here, of course,' said Alice with a frown.

'No, you won't,' said Tweedledee. 'You'll be nowhere. You're just a person in the Red King's dream. That's all.'

'If he wakes up,' added Tweedledum, 'you'll go out, like the flame of a candle!'

'I won't!' replied Alice. 'I'll still be here. I'm a real person.' She started to cry. Then she had a thought. She said, 'If I'm not real, I can't cry. And I *am* crying – so I *must* be real!'

'Ha!' said Tweedledum. 'Those aren't real tears.'

'They're talking nonsense,' thought Alice, drying her eyes on her handkerchief. 'It's silly to cry about it.'

It was getting dark in the forest and Alice could see black clouds in the sky. 'Do you think it will rain?' she asked the brothers.

Tweedledum opened a large umbrella. He held it above himself and Tweedledee. 'It won't rain under here,' he said.

'But will it rain out *here*?' asked Alice.

'If it does, we'll be dry under this umbrella,' replied Tweedledee.

'But *I'm* not under the umbrella! They don't care if *I* get wet,' thought Alice. 'They only care about themselves. I'll say goodbye and go.'

But then Tweedledum jumped forward and grabbed her hand. 'Look at that!' he cried. He pointed his finger at a small white thing which was lying on the ground.

Alice looked at it carefully. 'Don't be upset,' she said. 'It's just a rattle. Just a baby's toy. And it's broken.'

Tweedledum started to stamp his feet and pull his hair. 'Broken!' he cried.

Alice put her hand on his arm and said, 'Please don't be upset. It's just an old rattle.'

'It *isn't* old!' screamed Tweedledum. 'It's new – I bought it yesterday!' He looked at Tweedledee, who was trying to hide under the umbrella. 'And now it's broken! *He* broke it!

We must have a battle. Do you agree, Tweedledee?'

'Oh, all right,' said Tweedledee, looking at Alice. 'But *she* must help us to get ready for it.'

The two brothers walked off into the forest. After a few minutes, they were back, carrying lots of things. Alice could see pillows, blankets and rugs, tablecloths, trays and cooking pots.

'Can you pin things and tie strings and do up buttons?' Tweedledum asked Alice. 'We have to wear all these things for the battle.'

With Alice's help, and a lot of shouting, the brothers put on their 'armour' to protect them in the battle.

'Will you put my helmet on for me?' asked Tweedledum.

'It isn't a helmet – it's a cooking pot,' thought Alice, carefully putting it on his head. She tried not to laugh. And then, at last, they were ready.

'Do I look ill?' Tweedledum asked Alice.

'Perhaps,' she replied, trying to see his face through all the armour.

'I'm a very brave man,' he went on, 'and I like fighting. But today my head hurts.'

'And my tooth hurts!' said Tweedledee, who was listening. 'I feel much worse than you.'

'Perhaps you shouldn't have the battle today if you're both ill,' said Alice. She didn't want them to fight.

'Oh, we must have the battle,' said Tweedledum. 'But we don't need to fight for long. What time is it now?'

Tweedledee looked at his watch and said, 'It's half past four.'

'Let's fight until six o'clock. Then we can stop for dinner,' said Tweedledum.

'All right,' said Tweedledee, looking at Alice. 'And she can watch us. But don't come too close. I might hit you. When I'm fighting, I hit everything I can see!'

'*I* hit *everything*,' said Tweedledum, 'if I can see it or not!'

Alice laughed. 'Do you hit a lot of trees, here in the forest?' she asked.

Tweedledum looked around him and smiled. 'When we've finished fighting,' he said proudly, 'there will *be* no trees!'

'But you're only fighting about a rattle!' said Alice. 'It's not a very important thing, you know.'

'But it was a *new* rattle!' replied Tweedledum sadly.

Alice remembered the second verse of the song. 'I wish the monstrous crow would come,' she thought. 'Then they would stop.'

'We've only got one sword,' said Tweedledee to his brother. 'You can have the umbrella. It's quite sharp. And it's time to start the battle.'

It was now very dark in the forest. 'I think there will be a thunderstorm,' said Alice to herself. 'I can see a big black cloud. It's moving very fast – I think it's got wings!'

'It's the crow!' cried Tweedledum. 'It's the monstrous crow! Let's forget about the battle. Run, Tweedledee, as fast as you can!' And the two brothers ran off, leaving Alice alone.

Alice went further into the forest and stood under a tall tree. 'The crow can't get me here,' she thought. 'But I wish it would stop flapping its wings. It's so windy! Oh, here's someone's shawl! The wind has blown it away.' Alice caught the shawl and looked around for its owner.

CHAPTER 5

A sheep in a shop

Someone was running through the trees. It was the White Queen. She was coming towards Alice. She was running so fast that she was almost flying!

Alice went to meet the White Queen. 'Good afternoon,' she said. 'I've found this shawl. Is it yours?'

The White Queen nodded and put her hand out to take the shawl. Alice helped her to put it round her shoulders. 'She's very untidy,' she thought. 'Her crown isn't straight, her hair is tangled and there are pins everywhere!'

As the White Queen tried to put a pin in her shawl, Alice said, 'Shall I do that for you?'

'Oh, yes, please. I can't get it right,' replied the White Queen. 'I've pinned it here and I've pinned it there, but nothing fixes it.'

Alice pinned the shawl for her. Then she said, 'Shall I brush your hair now?'

'You'll have to get the brush out first. It's stuck

in my hair. And I lost my comb yesterday,' replied the White Queen.

Alice found the brush and started to tidy the White Queen's hair. Then she tidied her clothes and put her crown on straight.

'There! That looks better,' she said. 'But you're a Queen. Don't you have a servant to help you with your clothes and your hair?'

'*You* can be my servant,' replied the White Queen. 'I'll pay you two pennies every week and you can have jam on your bread!'

Alice started to laugh. 'I don't want to be your servant!' she said. 'And I don't want any jam!'

'It's very good jam,' said the White Queen with a frown.

'Well, I don't want any *today*,' said Alice.

'You can't have jam today. You can have jam yesterday, but never jam today. That's the rule,' cried the White Queen.

'I don't understand,' said Alice. 'It's all very confusing.'

'I live backwards, you see,' explained the White Queen. 'It *is* confusing at first.'

'But how can you live backwards?' asked poor Alice. 'No one can do that.'

'*I* can,' said the White Queen. 'I can remember things before they happen.'

'I can't,' said Alice. 'What sort of things do you remember?'

'Things that happened next week, mostly.' As she spoke, the White Queen took a bandage from her pocket and put it on her finger.

'Why is she doing that?' wondered Alice. 'She hasn't hurt herself.'

'Let me tell you about the King's Messenger,' said the White Queen. 'He's in prison, poor thing. Soon, of course, he'll do the crime. Backwards, you see.'

'But he may *not* do the crime,' said Alice.

'That would be a good thing, wouldn't it?' said the White Queen.

'It *would* be a good thing, but it wouldn't be a good thing if they punished him for it,' said Alice.

'Have you ever been punished?' asked the White Queen.

'Yes, of course. But not for something I didn't do!' said Alice.

'Well, if you didn't do it, that's even better!' said the White Queen. Suddenly, the White Queen started to scream: 'Oh! Oh! Oh!' She shook her hand. 'My finger hurts! Oh! Oh! Oh!'

'What's wrong?' asked Alice. 'Have you stuck a pin in your finger?'

'Not yet,' replied the White Queen. 'But I'll do it soon. Oh! Oh! Oh!'

'When will you do it?' asked Alice, trying not to laugh.

'When I pin my shawl again,' the White Queen replied. She took out the pin and started to stick it in her shawl. 'It's happened! The pin has slipped! Oh, my poor finger!' She smiled at Alice. 'That's how things happen here, you see. Everything goes backwards.'

The sky was much lighter now. 'I think the crow has gone,' said Alice. 'I'm pleased about that. But I'm so lonely here in Looking-glass Land.' She started to cry.

'Think about something and you'll feel better,' the White Queen told her. 'Think about the things you've done today. Think about what time it is. Think about anything!'

'Will that help?' asked Alice.

'Well, no one can do two things at the same time,' the White Queen replied. 'If you think about something, you won't be able to cry. Now, let's think about how old we are. How old are you?'

'I'm exactly ten and a half,' said Alice.

'Well, *I* am two hundred and one years, five months and one day,' said the White Queen.

'I can't believe that!' said Alice.

'Can't you? Shut your eyes and try again,' said the White Queen kindly.

'But it's impossible!' said Alice. 'I *can't* believe something that's impossible!'

'Oh, *I* can,' replied the White Queen. 'Sometimes I believe six impossible things before breakfast. Oh, my shawl has gone again!'

The wind had picked up the shawl and carried it over a little stream. The White Queen ran after it. She jumped over the stream and chased her shawl. Alice followed her over the stream and into the fifth square.

Alice looked for the White Queen, but she had gone. Alice decided to stop and rest.

Suddenly, she heard a noise: 'Baa! Baa!' It was coming from a small shop nearby. Alice walked over to the shop and went inside. It was dark and a sheep was sitting behind the counter, knitting. She was wearing glasses and a little cap.

Alice could see lots of different things – a fan, some spades, some hoops and even a kite. In the window, there were jars full of sweets and a toy horse.

The Sheep looked at Alice through her large round glasses.

'What do you want to buy?' she asked.

'I don't know yet,' replied Alice. 'I'd like to look all round me before I decide.'

'You can look in front of you and you can look to both sides. But you haven't got eyes in the back of your head, so you can't look all round you,' said the Sheep.

Alice started to walk round the shop. But as soon as she looked at a shelf, it became empty. All the other shelves were still full.

She tried to look at a pretty doll, but it moved to a higher shelf. It turned into a knitting basket and then it moved even higher.

'I'll follow it to the top shelf,' thought Alice. 'It will have to stop then – it can't go through the ceiling.' But it did!

'Will you stop that, please?' said the Sheep. 'You're making me dizzy.'

Alice was surprised to see that the Sheep was now knitting with fourteen needles.

'Can you row a boat?' asked the Sheep, giving Alice a pair of needles.

'Yes,' replied Alice. 'But not on land and not with knitting needles – oh!'

The needles had turned into oars and they were now sitting in a little boat on a river! Alice started to row with the oars. The boat moved slowly along. Alice saw some flowers growing by the river bank.

'Can we stop the boat for a minute?' she said. 'I'd like to pick some of those flowers – they're so pretty.' Alice put down the oars. She bent over the side of the boat and started to pick the flowers. Soon there was a big pile of them in the bottom of the boat.

'I've got enough now,' said Alice. She picked up the oars again and started to row. But then one of the oars got stuck in some plants under the water.

As Alice tried to pull it out, the other end caught her under the chin and pushed her off the seat. She fell onto the pile of flowers. The Sheep didn't help her. She didn't even stop knitting. But Alice was not hurt and she climbed back onto the seat.

'Now, what do you want to buy?' asked the Sheep. 'I've got lots of things – what would you like?'

The oars, the boat and the river had all disappeared. They were back in the little shop. Alice thought for a minute. Then she saw some eggs in a bowl on the counter. 'I'd like to buy an egg, please,' she said. 'How much are they?'

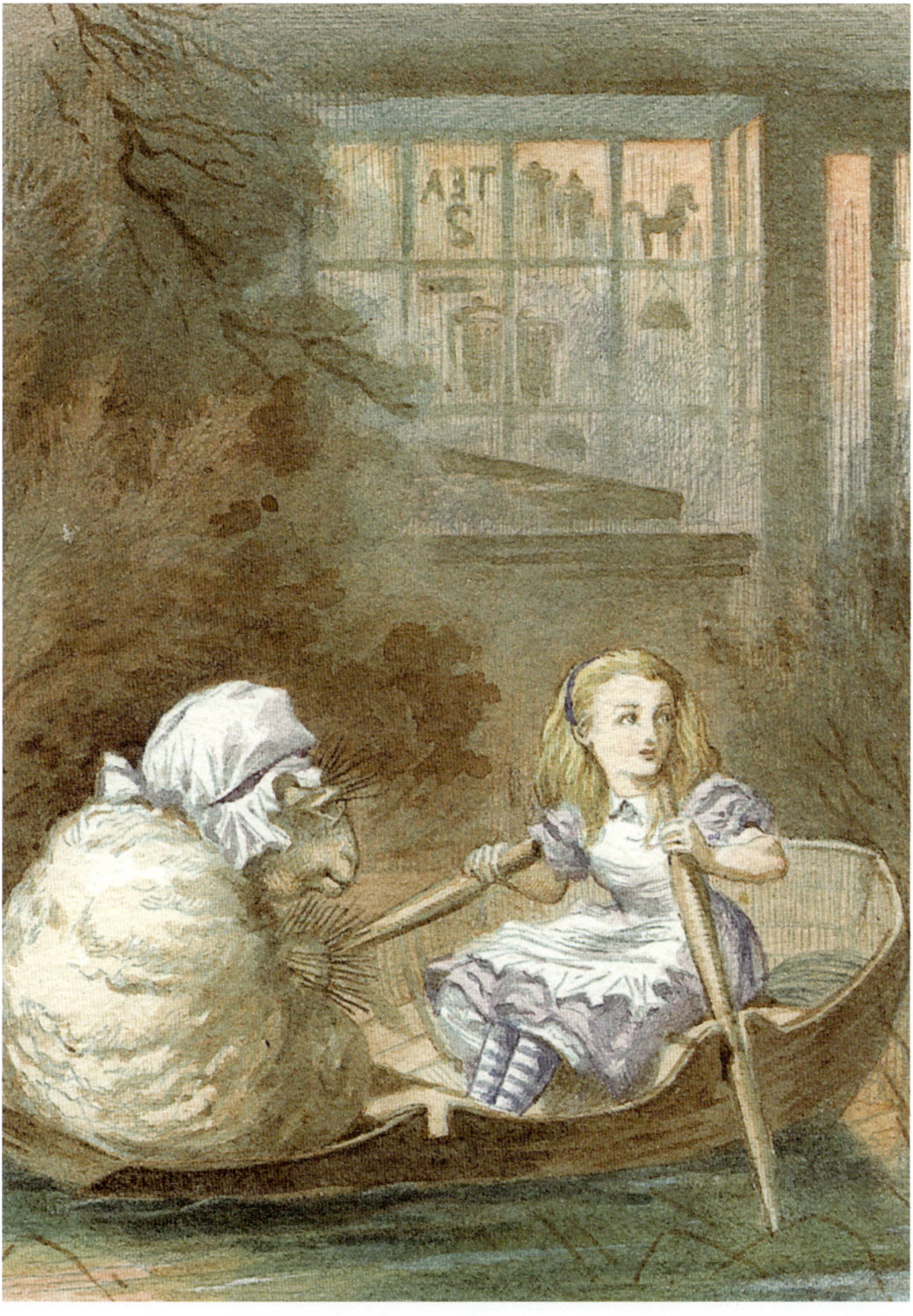

'Five pennies for one egg or two pennies for two eggs,' the Sheep replied.

'So two eggs are cheaper than one egg?' asked Alice, as she took her purse from her pocket. 'I don't understand.'

'And if you buy two,' the Sheep went on, 'you *must* eat them both now.'

'Then I'll only buy one,' said Alice. She gave the Sheep five pennies.

Alice stretched out her hand to take the egg. But the Sheep picked it up and took it to the other side of the shop. She put the egg on a shelf. 'I won't give it to you. You can get it yourself,' she said.

Alice walked towards the egg. But it seemed to move further and further away.

'It's very dark in here,' she said. 'Is this a chair? No, it's got branches. It's a tree! And here's a little stream! This is a very strange shop.'

Alice walked behind the egg as it went over the stream and into the sixth square.

CHAPTER 6

Humpty Dumpty

The egg got bigger and bigger. Then it stopped moving and now Alice could see that it had a big round face and arms and legs.

'I think it's Humpty Dumpty,' she said to herself.

He was sitting, with his legs crossed, on top of a very high wall.

'Oh, I hope you won't fall off,' said Alice. She stretched out her arms, ready to catch him. 'You're an egg – if you fall off the wall, you'll break.'

There was a long silence. Then Humpty Dumpty frowned and said, 'I'm not an egg. I'm Humpty Dumpty.'

'There's nothing wrong with eggs. Some eggs are very pretty, you know,' replied Alice.

'And some people,' said Humpty Dumpty, 'talk a lot of nonsense.'

Alice couldn't think of an answer to this. But she suddenly remembered a poem about Humpty Dumpty and she whispered it to herself:

Humpty Dumpty sat on a wall.
Humpty Dumpty had a great fall.
All the King's horses and all the King's men
Couldn't put Humpty together again.

'Oh, I hope that doesn't happen!' thought Alice.

Humpty Dumpty looked at her and said, 'Stop talking to yourself, child, and tell me your name.'

'My name's Alice,' she replied.

'That's a very silly name,' said Humpty Dumpty. 'What does it mean?'

'It doesn't mean anything!' said Alice. 'It's just a name.'

'*My* name means something,' said Humpty Dumpty. 'It tells you what shape I am. And I'm a very fine shape, you know. But if your name's Alice, you could be any shape.'

'I don't know what to say to that. I'll talk about something else,' thought Alice. She said, 'Why are you sitting here all alone?'

'That's easy,' said Humpty Dumpty. 'I'm all alone because nobody is with me!'

'But the wall is so high,' Alice said. 'Why don't you get down and sit on the ground? You would be much safer.'

'If I fall off,' said Humpty Dumpty proudly, 'I'll be all right. The White King has told me that he'll ...'

'... send all his horses and all his men!' Alice finished his sentence for him. But then she wished she had said nothing.

'How did you know that?' cried Humpty Dumpty. 'Who told you?'

'Nobody told me. I read it in a book,' said Alice.

'Oh, books! Pfff!' said Humpty Dumpty. He smiled at Alice. 'Now, look at me. As you know, I've spoken to a King, so I'm a very important person. You may shake my hand.'

With a wide smile, he leant down and held out his hand. Alice shook it. 'What a big smile,' she thought.

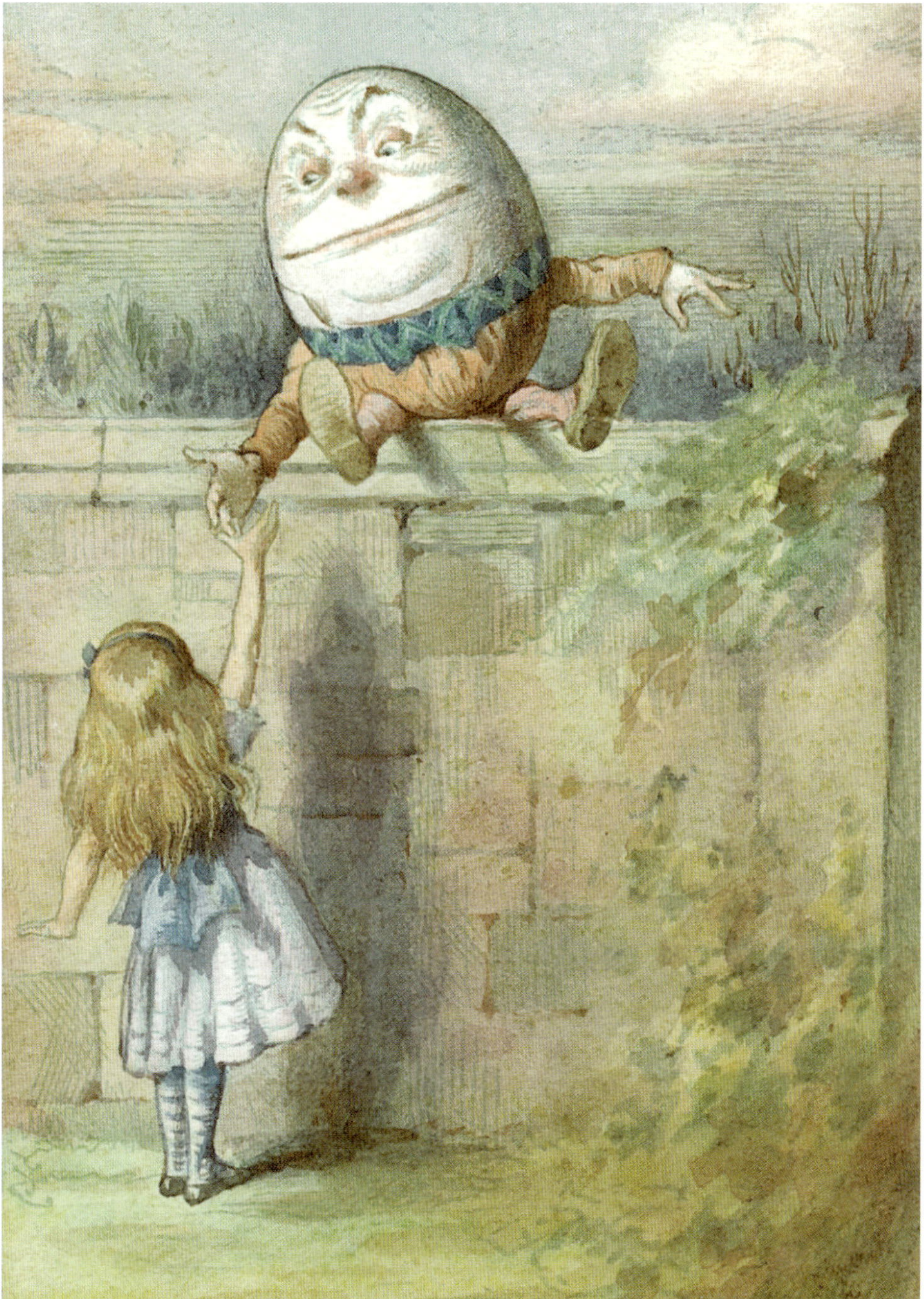

'If he smiles any more, the two ends of the smile will meet at the back! Then what will happen? Will his head fall off?'

'As I was saying,' Humpty Dumpty went on. 'All the King's horses and all the King's men. If I fall off this wall, they'll come and pick me up straight away! Now, here's a question for you. How old are you?'

'I'm ten and a half,' replied Alice.

'Ten and a half! That's not a very good age,' said Humpty Dumpty. He thought for a moment. 'You should have stopped getting older when you were ten.'

'What nonsense,' thought Alice. She said, 'I can't stop getting older. Nobody can do that.'

'That's enough about age,' she thought. 'I'll talk about something else.' She saw that Humpty Dumpty was wearing a bright green belt.

'What a beautiful belt!' she said to him. Then she looked at it again and her face turned red. 'Oh! I mean, what a beautiful bow tie!'

Humpty Dumpty looked angry and there was silence for a few minutes.

'Oh, dear. I think I've upset him,' thought Alice. 'But is it a belt or is it a bow tie? Which is his body and which is his neck? I really don't know. He's so round!'

'I'm very sorry,' she said.

After a minute, Humpty Dumpty replied, 'It's a bow tie, of course, not a belt. They're quite different, you know. And it's a very beautiful bow tie. It was a present from the White King and the White Queen. It was an unbirthday present.'

Alice frowned. 'I've never heard of an unbirthday present. What is it?' she asked.

'It's a present that you get when it isn't your birthday. It's much better than a birthday present. Tell me, how many days are there in a year?' asked Humpty Dumpty.

'I know the answer to that. Three hundred and sixty-five,' Alice replied.

'And how many birthdays do you have in a year?' asked Humpty Dumpty.

'One,' said Alice.

'If you subtract one from three hundred and sixty-five, what do you get?' he asked next.

'Three hundred and sixty-four,' said Alice.

'Will you write that down for me, please?' asked Humpty Dumpty.

Alice smiled and took her notebook from her pocket. She wrote:

$$\begin{array}{r} 365 \\ -1 \\ \hline 364 \end{array}$$

Humpty Dumpty took the notebook and looked at it. 'I think that's right ...' he said, 'but I'm not very good at maths.'

'It's upside down!' laughed Alice, turning the notebook round for him.

'Well, as you can see, you have three hundred and sixty-four unbirthdays and only one birthday!' cried Humpty Dumpty. 'Which is better?'

'Perhaps you're right,' replied Alice. 'Three hundred and sixty-four presents would be better than just one.'

'And now I'm going to sing a song,' said Humpty Dumpty. 'I've written it just for you. Please sit down and listen.'

Alice sat on the ground and he began:

*In winter, when the fields are white,
I sing this song for your delight.*

*In spring, when woods are getting green,
I'll try and tell you what I mean.*

*In summer, when the days are long,
Perhaps you'll understand the song.*

*In autumn, when the leaves are brown,
Take pen and ink, and write it down.*

Humpty Dumpty stopped singing.
'Is that the end?' asked Alice.
'Yes, it is,' he replied. 'Goodbye.'
Surprised, Alice stood up and held out her hand. 'Goodbye, until we meet again,' she said.
Humpty Dumpty shook her hand and said, 'If we *do* meet again, I won't know who you are.'
'But you will if you look at my face,' Alice replied.
'Oh, faces are all the same,' said Humpty Dumpty. 'Everyone has two eyes at the top, a nose in the middle and a mouth at the bottom. Now, if your mouth was at the top of your face …'
'It would look very strange,' said Alice.
But Humpty Dumpty just shut his eyes and said no more.

'I think it's time to go,' thought Alice. 'I'm glad he didn't fall off the wall.' She walked off into the forest.

Then Alice heard a loud crash behind her. When she turned round, she saw soldiers running through the forest. First they came in twos and threes, and then they came in tens and twenties. Soon the forest was full of soldiers.

'It's the King's men!' thought Alice. 'They've come to help Humpty Dumpty. I'll hide behind this tree and watch.'

One soldier fell over a tree root. Then another one fell. This happened again and again, and soon all the soldiers were lying on the ground.

Then some horses arrived with more soldiers on their backs. Like the men, the horses fell down and all the riders fell off.

'What a mess!' thought Alice, as she walked away from them all.

CHAPTER 7

The Lion and the Unicorn

Soon Alice came to a large space between the trees. She saw a road leading out of the forest. Someone was sitting on the ground, writing in a notebook. It was the White King! Alice went closer.

When he saw Alice, the White King smiled at her and said, 'Did you see any soldiers in the forest?'

'Yes, I did,' replied Alice. 'I saw thousands of them.'

The White King looked in his notebook. 'Four thousand, two hundred and seven!' he said. 'I sent them to help Humpty. I wanted to send my two Messengers as well, but they went to the town. Are they coming back yet? Can you see them?'

Alice shaded her eyes with her hand and looked down the road. 'I can see nobody,' she replied.

'Can you really?' cried the White King. 'And he's so far away! You have very good eyes. I wish I could see Nobody. Sometimes I can't even see real people.'

Alice was still looking along the road. 'I can see someone now!' she cried. 'But he's coming very slowly. He's skipping and wriggling like a fish and flapping his hands.'

'Oh, he does that when he's Happy,' replied the White King. 'His name is Haigha, which rhymes with "chair". He eats Hay and he lives on a Hill. My other Messenger is called Hatta. I need two Messengers, you see. One to come and one to go.'

As Alice was thinking about this, Haigha arrived. He was panting and waving his arms at the White King. He wriggled and rolled his eyes round and round.

'Will you stop that?' said the White King. 'I feel quite ill now. I think I need a honey sandwich. Have you got one in your bag?'

Haigha opened the bag that hung round his neck and took out a honey sandwich. He gave it to the White King, who ate it greedily and then said, 'May I have another?'

Haigha looked in his bag again. 'I'm sorry,' he said. 'There's only hay in here.'

'Then give me some hay,' whispered the White King, closing his eyes. When he had eaten some hay, he opened his eyes and said, 'I feel much better now. Hay is the best thing when you feel ill.'

Alice didn't agree with this. 'I think cold water would be better,' she said.

The White King looked at Haigha. 'Who did you pass on the road?' he asked.

'I passed nobody,' the Messenger replied.

'Ah, Nobody!' cried the White King. 'This child saw him, too! So Nobody walks more slowly than you.'

'That's not true,' said Haigha, rolling his eyes. 'Nobody walks more quickly than I do.'

'Then why didn't he arrive first?' asked the White King.

Poor Haigha had no answer to this.

Then the White King said, 'What's happening in the town, Haigha?'

'I'll whisper it to you,' replied Haigha. He made his hands into the shape of a trumpet and bent down to whisper in the White King's ear.

'Please don't whisper,' thought Alice. 'I'd like to hear it.'

So she was pleased when Haigha shouted, 'They're fighting again!'

'That's not whispering!' cried the White King. He covered his ears and jumped up and down. 'It sounded like an earthquake!'

'A very small earthquake,' thought Alice. '*Who* is fighting again?' she asked.

'The Lion and the Unicorn, of course,' replied the White King. 'They're going to fight for the crown. *My* crown! Shall we go and watch them?'

'Yes, all right,' Alice replied.

As they ran along the road to the town, Alice remembered a song and started to sing it:

The Lion and the Unicorn were fighting for the crown.
The Lion beat the Unicorn all around the town.
Some gave them white bread, some gave them brown,
Some gave them plum cake and drummed them out of town.

'Will the winner get the crown?' she asked.

'No,' replied the White King. 'What an idea! It's *my* crown!'

When they came to the town, Alice saw a large crowd. In the middle of it, the Lion and the Unicorn were fighting.

'But which is the Lion and which is the Unicorn?' wondered Alice. 'They're making so much dust that I can't see. Oh, now I can see a long pointed horn. That must be the Unicorn.'

Then Haigha said, 'This is Hatta, the other Messenger.'

Alice looked at Hatta. He was holding a cup of tea in one hand and a piece of bread and butter in the other.

'He's just come out of prison,' Haigha went on. 'He was having his tea when he went in. How are you, dear boy?' He put his arm round Hatta's neck.

Hatta just nodded and drank some tea.

'Who's winning the fight?' the White King asked him.
'The Unicorn is winning this time,' replied Hatta. 'They've been fighting for a long time.'

'Is it time for the bread?' asked Alice, remembering the song.

'Yes,' said Hatta. 'It's all ready. I'm eating a piece of the white bread now.'

The Lion and the Unicorn stopped fighting and sat down.

The White King called out, 'Ten minutes for bread and butter, everyone!'

Haigha and Hatta carried round trays of white and brown bread, and everyone ate a piece.

Then the White King said to Hatta, 'They won't fight any more today. Go and tell the drums to begin.'

Alice wondered about the drums as she watched Hatta run off. Then, far away, she saw someone else.

'Look! It's the White Queen,' she cried. 'She's running through the forest. Those Queens can run very fast.'

'She's running away from one of her enemies,' said the White King. 'The forest is full of them.'

'But won't you go and help her?' asked Alice.

'Oh, no,' he replied. 'She runs much too fast for me. But I'll write a note about her in my notebook.' He took out his notebook and started to write.

The Unicorn came up to them with his hands in his pockets. 'I won the fight this time,' he said to the White King. Then he saw Alice.

'Who's this?' he asked, staring at her quite rudely, Alice thought.

'It's a child!' said Haigha, waving his arms at Alice. 'A human child! We found her today.'

'But I thought children were monsters,' replied the Unicorn with a snort. 'Not real – just pretend. Is she alive?'

'Oh, yes,' said Haigha.

'Can she talk?' asked the Unicorn.

'She can,' said Haigha.

'Then talk, child!' cried the Unicorn.

Alice started to smile. 'Well, *I* have never seen a *unicorn* before,' she said. 'I thought unicorns were monsters. Not real – just pretend.'

'Let's agree, then,' said the Unicorn. 'I'll believe that you're real if you'll believe that I am.'

'Yes, all right,' said Alice.

The Unicorn turned to the White King. 'Let's have some plum cake,' he said. 'I don't like bread.'

Haigha opened his bag and looked inside.

'Not that bag,' said the White King. 'There's only hay in that one. Look in the other bag.'

So Haigha took out the plum cake, a long knife and a very large plate. 'Will you hold it?' he asked Alice.

'All those things in one little bag,' thought Alice as she took the cake. 'It's like a magic trick!'

Then the Lion arrived, looking very sleepy. 'Who are you?' he asked Alice with a yawn.

Before she could reply, the Unicorn said, 'She's a monster. She's not real – she's just pretend.'

The Lion lay down and put his head on his paws. 'Will you cut up the cake, Monster?' he asked. 'Sit down, everyone.'

So they all sat down and Alice picked up the knife.

'I'll win the next fight,' growled the Lion to the Unicorn. 'Last time, I beat you all around the town.'

The Unicorn stared at the White King's crown. 'Oh, no, you won't. I'll win,' he said angrily.

The King started to shake – he was sitting between the two great fighters and he felt frightened. 'Please don't quarrel,' he said. 'Did you go through the market or past the old bridge?' he asked the Lion.

The Lion grunted. 'I don't know,' he said. 'It was too dusty to see anything.' Then he said to Alice, 'Have you cut up the cake yet, Monster?'

Alice was sitting by a little stream with the cake in her lap. 'I'm trying,' she said. 'But it's very difficult. I've cut four slices – but now they're joined to the cake again!'

'Remember, it's a Looking-glass cake,' said the Unicorn. 'You must pass it round first and then cut it up.'

'That's nonsense,' thought Alice, but she decided to try it. She passed the cake round. As she did so, it cut itself into slices and everybody took one.

'*Now* cut it up,' said the Unicorn. Alice looked at the empty plate, wondering what to do.

'The Lion's got the biggest slice,' the Unicorn said to Alice. 'It's not fair.'

But before she could reply, the drums started to play.

CHAPTER 8

The White Knight

The sound of the drums filled the air.

'It's too noisy for me here,' thought Alice. 'It's time to go now.' She jumped up and crossed the little stream into the seventh square. When she looked back, she could see the Lion and the Unicorn. They looked angry because the drums had spoiled their picnic.

Alice could still hear the drums. She put her hands over her ears to shut out the noise. '*That* will soon drum them out of town,' she said to herself.

At last the drums stopped. When Alice looked back, she couldn't see the Lion or the Unicorn. She couldn't see Haigha or Hatta. Had she dreamed them? But when she looked down, she saw that the cake plate was still in her hand.

'So it wasn't a dream,' she said to herself. She walked away, still holding the plate.

Then she heard a shout and a Red Knight galloped towards her on his horse. 'You're my prisoner!' he cried.

Then there was another shout and a White Knight rode up to them. The two Knights looked at each other.

'She's *my* prisoner,' said the Red Knight.

'And *I* came to rescue her,' replied the White Knight.

'Then we must fight for her!' cried the Red Knight. He put on his helmet, which was the shape of a horse's head.

The two Knights started to fight and Alice watched from behind a tree. 'Oh dear, more fighting,' she thought sadly.

It was a very noisy battle. If one Knight hit the other Knight, that one fell off his horse. If he missed, he fell off his own horse. In the end, both Knights fell off their horses, landing on their heads. They stood up and shook hands. Then the Red Knight jumped onto his horse and galloped away.

'I'm the winner!' cried the White Knight.

'And *I'm* not a prisoner,' said Alice. 'I'm pleased about that. But I really want to be a Queen.'

'You *will* be a Queen,' the White Knight replied, 'when you get to the eighth square. Now, I'll go with you to the edge of the forest and then I must leave you. Knights can't go further than that.'

'Thank you very much,' said Alice. 'Shall I help you to take off your helmet?'

Taking off the horse-shaped helmet took quite a long time. When at last it was off, the White Knight pushed back his hair and Alice looked at him carefully.

'He's very strange,' thought Alice. 'His eyes are so large and his hair is so long.' Then she noticed a small wooden box, hanging upside down from his armour. The lid was open.

'Do you like my little box?' asked the White Knight. 'I invented it myself. I keep my clothes and my sandwiches in it. It hangs upside down to keep the rain out.'

'But the things in the box will fall out,' said Alice. 'The lid is open.'

'Is it? Then all my things *have* fallen out,' replied the White Knight sadly. 'So I don't need the box any more. I'll throw it into the bushes.' He untied it, but then he said, 'No, I won't throw it away. I'll hang it on this tree. Bees may make a nest in it. Then I could have some honey. I like honey.'

Alice frowned. 'But you already have a beehive,' she said. 'I can see it. It's tied to your saddle.'

'Yes, and it's a very good beehive,' replied the White Knight. 'It's the best sort. But there are no bees in it. They never come. And the other thing is a mousetrap. The mice keep the bees away and the bees keep the mice away.'

'But there won't be any mice,' said Alice. 'Not on a horse's back.'

'We don't know that. Some mice *may* come,' said the White Knight. 'And if they do, the mousetrap is ready for them. I like to be ready for anything. That's why my horse has spikes fixed to his legs. I invented them myself. They're to keep sharks away, you see.'

Alice tried not to laugh. 'Sharks, in a forest?' she thought.

'And now it's time to go,' the White Knight said. He climbed onto his horse and they set off. After a few minutes, the White Knight said, 'Why are you carrying that plate?'

'It's a cake plate,' replied Alice. 'It's for plum cake.'

'Help me to put it in this bag,' said the White Knight. 'If we find any plum cake, we'll need it.'

It was difficult to get the plate into the bag because there were so many spoons in it. But at last it was in. The White Knight hung it on his saddle with a bunch of carrots and many other things.

As they went through the forest, the White Knight said, 'The wind can be very strong, you know. Is your hair fixed tightly on your head?'

'Yes, I think so,' said Alice with a smile. 'Have you invented a way to stop it blowing off?'

'Not yet,' replied the White Knight. 'But I *have* invented a way to stop hair falling out. You can try it if you like.'

'Tell me about it,' said Alice.

'You must take a straight stick and put it on your head,' the White Knight explained. 'Then you make your hair grow up it. Hair falls out because it hangs *down*, you see. But nothing can fall upwards.'

Alice thought about this strange idea as they went through the forest.

The White Knight was not a very good rider. He fell off his horse again and again, and each time Alice had to help him to get back on. After the fifth time, Alice said, 'I don't think you've ridden many horses.'

'Why do you say that?' asked the White Knight with a frown.

'Because you fall off so often,' replied Alice.

'I've ridden lots of horses!' cried the White Knight. He shut his eyes and started whispering to himself.

'Oh, I've upset him,' thought Alice.

After a few minutes, the White Knight waved his arm in the air and said, 'A good rider always ...'

He stopped speaking suddenly and fell off his horse. He landed on his head.

'Are you all right?' asked Alice as she helped him to get up. 'Have you broken any bones?'

'Oh, only a few,' he replied. 'As I was saying, a good rider always keeps his balance. Like this.' He dropped the reins and stretched out his arms. Then he fell off again. 'Lots of horses. Lots of horses,' he said, as Alice helped him to climb up again.

'This is all very silly,' she said. 'You should have a rocking horse. It would be much easier to ride.'

'Do rocking horses go very smoothly?' asked the White Knight, holding tightly onto his horse's neck.

'They go more smoothly than real ones,' laughed Alice.

'Then I'll get one,' said the White Knight. 'Or two, perhaps.'

They went on in silence. Then the White Knight said, 'I've invented a way of getting over a gate. Shall I tell you about it?'

'Yes, please,' said Alice.

'Well,' said the White Knight, 'if you're standing up, your head is high enough to get over the gate. But your feet are too low. So if you put your head on the gate and then put your feet up in the air, you can do it!'

'But that would be very difficult,' said Alice. 'Have you tried it?'

'Not yet,' he replied. 'But I'll try it soon ...' Then he fell off his horse again and into a deep hole. He went in head first, with his legs waving in the air, but he didn't stop talking.

Alice pulled him out. 'How can you talk when your head is in a hole?' she asked.

'I never stop thinking and inventing things,' he said. 'And I like to talk about my inventions. I do it better when I'm upside down.'

Soon they came to the edge of the forest.

'I must go back now,' said the White Knight as he pulled on the reins to turn his horse. 'But you're nearly there. Go down the hill and over a little stream, and then you'll be in the eighth square. Soon you'll be a Queen! But will you wait here until I get to that bend in the path? Will you wave your hand to say goodbye?'

'Yes, of course I will,' said Alice. 'And thank you for coming so far with me.'

They shook hands and Alice watched the White Knight as he rode slowly back into the forest. He fell off five more times. When at last he reached the bend in the path, Alice waved to him. Then he was gone.

'Now for the eighth square,' said Alice to herself. 'Then I can be a Queen.' She started to run down the hill.

Soon she came to the little stream and she jumped over it. Then she sat down to rest. She was sitting on soft green grass and she could see lots of beautiful flowers. 'I'm so pleased to be here at last,' she said to herself. 'But there's something on my head – what is it?'

She put her hands up to feel it. It was heavy and smooth, and it fitted tightly round her head. She lifted it off and looked at it. It was a gold crown. Alice laughed and put the crown back on her head. 'Now you're Queen Alice,' she said to herself. 'But you mustn't sit on the grass, Your Majesty. Stand up straight, hold your head up and be a real Queen!'

CHAPTER 9

Queen Alice

Alice walked up and down on the grass with the gold crown on her head. 'I hope it won't fall off,' she said to herself. 'That would never happen to a real Queen. But if it does fall off, no one will see it.' She sat down again. 'I just need to practise,' she thought. 'If I really am a Queen, I'll get it right in the end.'

Then she saw the White Queen and the Red Queen sitting together on the grass. 'I wonder if the game of chess has finished,' she thought. 'I'll ask them.'

'Please can you tell me ...' she began.

But the Red Queen said, 'Be quiet, child! Only speak when someone has spoken to you!'

'That's silly,' said Alice. 'If everyone did that, no one would ever speak!'

The Red Queen frowned as she thought about this. Then she said, 'Do you really think you're a Queen just because you're wearing a crown? Well, you're not. Not yet. All Queens must pass a test. You can take it now.'

Then the Red Queen turned to the White Queen. 'By the way, I invite you to Alice's party this afternoon,' she said.

'And I invite *you*,' replied the White Queen with a smile.

'Oh, am I going to have a party?' asked Alice. 'I didn't know. Well, I think I should invite the guests, not you.'

'You're very rude,' said the Red Queen. 'Didn't your teacher give you lessons in manners?'

'Children don't have lessons in manners,' replied Alice. 'They have lessons in maths and things like that.'

'Let's do the test now,' said the White Queen. 'We'll see if you can remember what you've learnt. We'll start with maths – addition, I think. What's one and one and one and one and one and one and one and one and one?'

'I don't know,' said Alice. 'You said it too fast.'

'She doesn't know!' cried the Red Queen. 'Well, she can't do addition.' She turned to Alice. 'Can you do subtraction? Subtract nine from eight.'

'I can't subtract nine from eight,' said Alice, 'because …'

'She can't do subtraction!' said the White Queen. 'We'll try division next. Divide a loaf of bread with a knife. What do you get?'

Alice had to think about this. But while she was thinking, the Red Queen gave the answer: 'Bread and butter, of course! Now we'll try another subtraction one. If you take a bone from a dog, what is left?'

'Well, the bone wouldn't be left because the dog would eat it. The dog wouldn't be left because it would come to bite me. And I wouldn't be left because I'd run away,' said Alice.

'So you think nothing would be left?' asked the Red Queen.

'I think that's the answer,' said Alice.

'You're wrong, again!' cried the Red Queen. 'You can't do maths at all!'

Alice felt very unhappy. 'Can *you* do maths?' she asked the White Queen.

'I can do addition,' she replied, 'if you give me enough time. But I can't do subtraction – oh, no, not at all!'

'Do you know your ABC?' the Red Queen asked Alice.

'Yes, of course I do,' she replied.

The White Queen said, 'I know my ABC, too. And I'll tell you a secret: I can read words with only one letter! Isn't that clever? You can do it, too, if you practise.'

'What else do you know?' the Red Queen asked Alice. 'Can you tell me how bread is made?'

'Well,' said Alice, 'you take some **flour** ...'

'But where do you *pick* the **flower**?' asked the White Queen. 'In a garden or in a field?'

'You don't *pick* the flour,' said Alice.

'You're leaving out too many things,' said the White Queen. 'Do you feel ill after thinking so much?'

The two Queens fanned Alice's face with leaves until she asked them to stop.

Then the White Queen said, 'She's all right now. I'll ask her another question: Which comes first, thunder or lightning?'

'I know the answer to that,' Alice thought. 'Well, I think I do.' She said, 'It's thunder. No – that's not right – it's lightning.'

'You can't change your answer,' said the Red Queen. 'Wrong again.'

'We had a big thunderstorm in the last set of Tuesdays,' said the White Queen.

'I don't understand,' said Alice. 'In my country, we only have one Tuesday each week.'

'Here,' said the Red Queen, 'we have two or three Tuesdays in a row. We have two or three nights in a row, too. Sometimes, in the winter, we have five nights in a row so we can keep warm.'

'Are five nights warmer than one night?' asked Alice.

'Five times as warm!' said the Red Queen.'

'But they should be five times as *cold*!' replied poor Alice.

'That's right!' cried the Red Queen. 'Five times as warm and five times as cold! Just as I'm five times as rich as you – and five times as clever!'

Alice sighed.

Then the Red Queen said, 'Humpty Dumpty visited me this morning.'

'What did he want?' asked the White Queen.

'He was looking for an elephant. But we didn't have any. We only have elephants on Thursdays,' said the Red Queen.

Suddenly, the White Queen started shouting. 'It was a terrible storm. The roof came off and the thunder got in. It went around the room and knocked all the chairs over!'

The Red Queen took one of the White Queen's hands and stroked it gently. 'She's tired, poor thing,' she told Alice. 'When she's tired, she says silly things. But she's very friendly. Pat her on the head – she likes that.'

'I can't pat a Queen on the head!' thought Alice.

The White Queen sighed and put her head in Alice's lap. 'I'm so sleepy,' she whispered.

'Stroke her hair,' said the Red Queen, 'and I'll sing to her until she's asleep:

Hush-a-bye lady, in Alice's lap!
Till the feast's ready, we've time for a nap.
When the feast's over, we'll go to the ball –
Red Queen, and White Queen, and Alice and all!'

Then she said to Alice, 'I'm tired, too. You know the song now, so I can go to sleep and you can sing it to both of us.'

Soon, both Queens were fast asleep and snoring loudly.

'What shall I do now?' said Alice to herself. 'Has anyone else looked after two Queens in all the history of England? I don't think so because we only have one Queen at a time.'

The White Queen's head was in Alice's lap and the Red Queen was leaning on her.

'Oh, wake up! You're both too heavy!' Alice said. But the only reply was more snoring. As Alice listened, it started to turn into a song.

When the song finished, the two Queens disappeared and Alice was standing in front of a door.

CHAPTER 10

Alice's party

Alice could hear lots of people singing. She stood on the doorstep and listened.

To the Looking-glass Land it was Alice that said,
'Look at me, I'm a Queen, I have a crown on my head.
Let the Looking-glass animals, whatever they be,
Come and dine with the Red Queen, the White Queen and me!'

Alice walked through the door and the singing stopped. She looked around her. She was in a large room with a long table in the middle of it. About fifty guests were sitting at the table – people, animals, birds and even some flowers. At the end of the table sat the Red Queen and the White Queen, with an empty chair between them.

'That must be my chair,' thought Alice, and she sat down. 'But I wish someone would say something.'

Then the Red Queen spoke. 'You're very late,' she said. 'You've missed the soup and the fish. It's time for the meat now. You can cut it up.'

One of the waiters put a large leg of lamb on the table in front of Alice.

'I've never done this before,' said Alice to herself as she picked up a knife. 'I hope it's not too difficult.'

Then the Red Queen said, 'Alice, I'd like you to meet the leg of lamb. Leg of lamb, this is Alice.'

The leg of lamb stood up in its dish and bowed to Alice.

'Should I laugh or should I be frightened?' Alice wondered. She bowed to the leg of lamb and then she said to the Red Queen, 'Would you like a piece?'

'No, I would not!' cried the Red Queen. 'Now that you've met the leg of lamb, you can't cut it up. That's very bad manners! Take it away, waiter!'

The waiter carried the leg of lamb away and came back with a large plum pudding.

'I don't want to talk to it – I want to eat it,' thought Alice. She was feeling hungry now. 'Would you like a piece?' she asked the Red Queen.

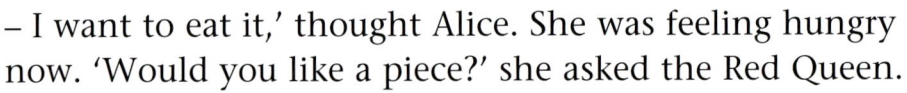

But the Red Queen said very quickly, 'Alice, meet the pudding. Pudding, meet Alice. Now take it away!' The pudding bowed and it was taken away.

Alice frowned. '*I* will give an order now!' she decided. 'Waiter – bring back the pudding!'

The waiter brought the pudding back to the table. Alice cut off a piece and gave it to the Red Queen.

'That was very rude!' cried the pudding. 'Would you like *me* to cut off a piece of *you*?'

There was silence. Then the Red Queen said, 'Say something, somebody! Don't let the pudding do all the talking!'

The White Queen said, 'Now we'll all drink to Queen Alice. Pick up your glasses, everyone!' She lifted her glass to her lips. 'To Queen Alice!' she cried.

All the guests drank, but in very strange ways. Some poured the juice onto their heads and drank it as it dripped down their faces. Some pushed the bottles over and drank the juice as it dripped off the table.

'And now,' said the Red Queen to Alice, 'you must make a speech.'

Alice stood up, suddenly feeling very shy. 'I'd like to thank you all for coming ...' she began.

But the two Queens were pushing her, one on each side. They pushed so hard that they lifted her off her chair.

And then the White Queen grabbed Alice's hair with both hands and shouted, 'Be careful! I think something's going to happen!'

First, the candles on the table grew so tall that they reached the ceiling. The flames looked like fireworks! Next, all the bottles turned into birds, with plates for wings and forks for legs.

Alice heard the White Queen laughing. She turned to her, but the leg of lamb was sitting in her chair. And the White Queen was smiling at her from the soup pot! 'Here I am!' she cried and disappeared into the soup.

The soup spoon was walking along the table towards Alice, looking very angry. It wanted Alice to move.

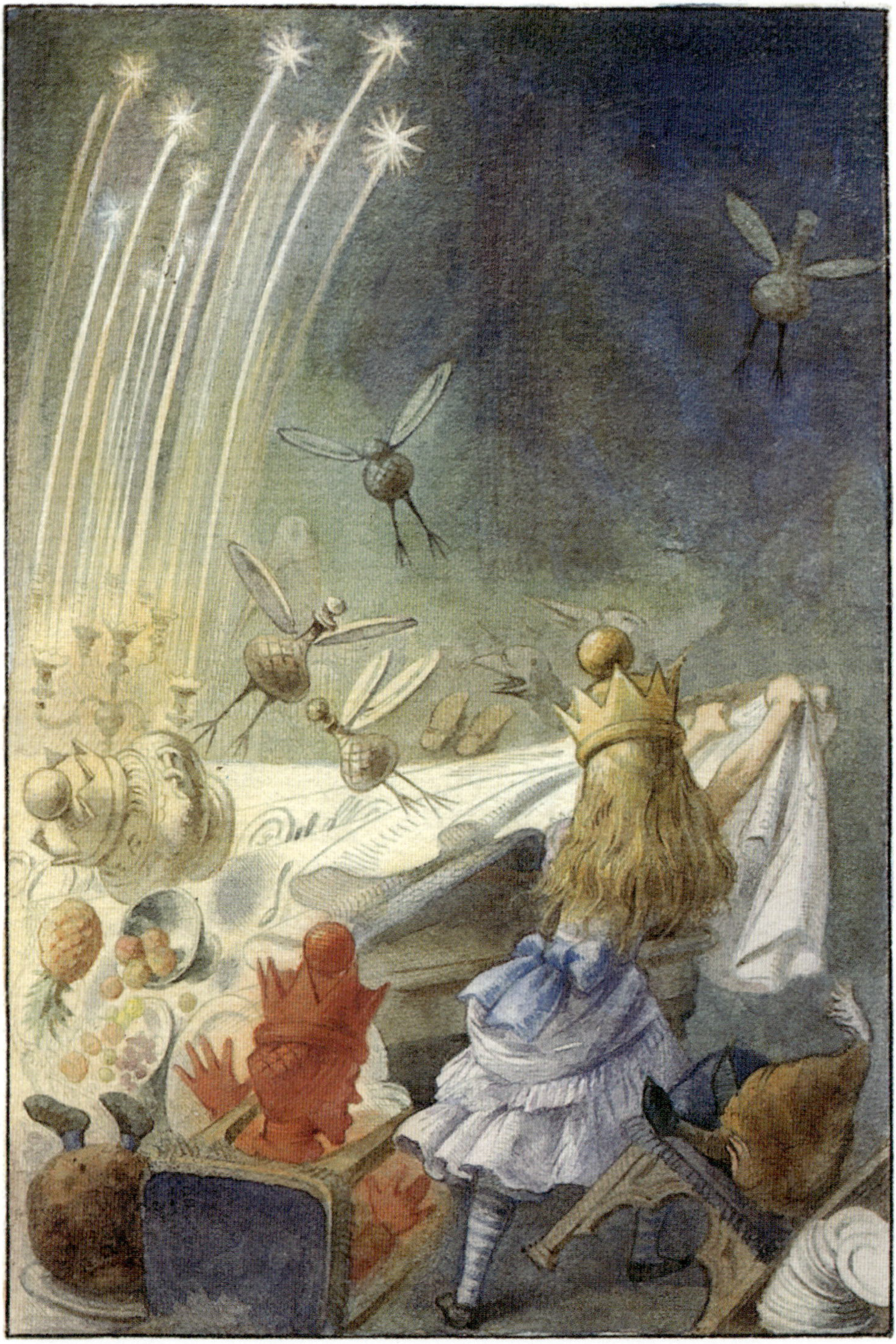

'Stop!' cried Alice. She stood up and grabbed the tablecloth with both hands. She pulled hard and everything – plates, dishes, guests, candles, spoons – crashed to the floor. Then she turned to the Red Queen, saying, 'You've done this, you ...'

But the Red Queen was now running round and round on the table, chasing after her shawl. She was as small as a doll. Alice grabbed her, just as she was about to jump over a bottle.

'I'll turn you into – a kitten!' cried Alice.

The Red Queen's eyes slowly turned green and she became fatter and softer and rounder and blacker, until she really was a kitten!

Alice rubbed her eyes and stroked the kitten. 'You're purring too loudly, Your Majesty,' she said sleepily. 'You woke me from a lovely dream. I've been in Looking-glass Land and you were there with me! Do you remember?'

The kitten didn't reply; she just purred.

'Do you mean yes or no?' asked Alice. 'Could you purr for yes and mew for no?'

But the kitten just purred. 'I don't know if you remember or not, Kitty,' sighed Alice. She stood up and went over to the table where the chess pieces stood. She found the Red Queen and put her on the floor next to the kitten.

'You turned into the Red Queen, Kitty,' she said. 'Do you remember?'

The kitten turned her head away and closed her eyes.

Alice laughed. 'Sit up straight, Kitty,' she said. 'And don't forget to bow!' She picked up the kitten and kissed her. 'You *did* turn into the Red Queen,' she said.

Then she turned to Snowdrop, the white kitten. Dinah was still washing the kitten's face.

'And you were the *White* Queen,' said Alice. 'You were untidy then and you're untidy now – poor Dinah is still washing you. Dinah, you're washing a Queen, you know! Who did *you* turn into, Dinah? Was it Humpty Dumpty?

'Now, Kitty, stop washing your paw. I have a question for you. Someone had a very strange dream, but who was it? The Red King was in my dream – but I was in his! So who dreamed it? Was it the Red King or was it me? Please tell me!'

But Kitty didn't reply. She just finished washing her paw, and then she lay down and closed her eyes.

So who had the dream? What do *you* think?

Left or right?

Mirror, mirror, on the wall?
Am I short or am I tall?

Now, what colour is my hair?
Is it dark or is it fair?
Is it short or is it long?
I know a mirror's never wrong.

And now my eyes – green, brown or blue?
To find out, I must look at you.

I've got an apple in my hand.
(This question is quite tricky and
I hope that you will get it right.)
So now, before I take a bite,
Which hand? Is it left or right?

Gill Munton

Chess

Alice's adventures in *Through the Looking-glass* are set on a giant chessboard.

Chess is a game for two players. Each player has sixteen pieces, which are red (or black) and white.

The players move their pieces around the squares on the board. Each piece moves in a different way. A Pawn starts in the second row of squares. It can move one or two squares in its first move. When a Pawn reaches the last row of squares (the eighth row), it turns into a Queen. Alice starts as a Pawn and becomes a Queen at the end.

The Queen is the most useful (and dangerous) piece because it can move in any direction.

The winner is the player who traps the other player's King so that it cannot move. This is called 'checkmate'.

THE BOARD

THE PIECES

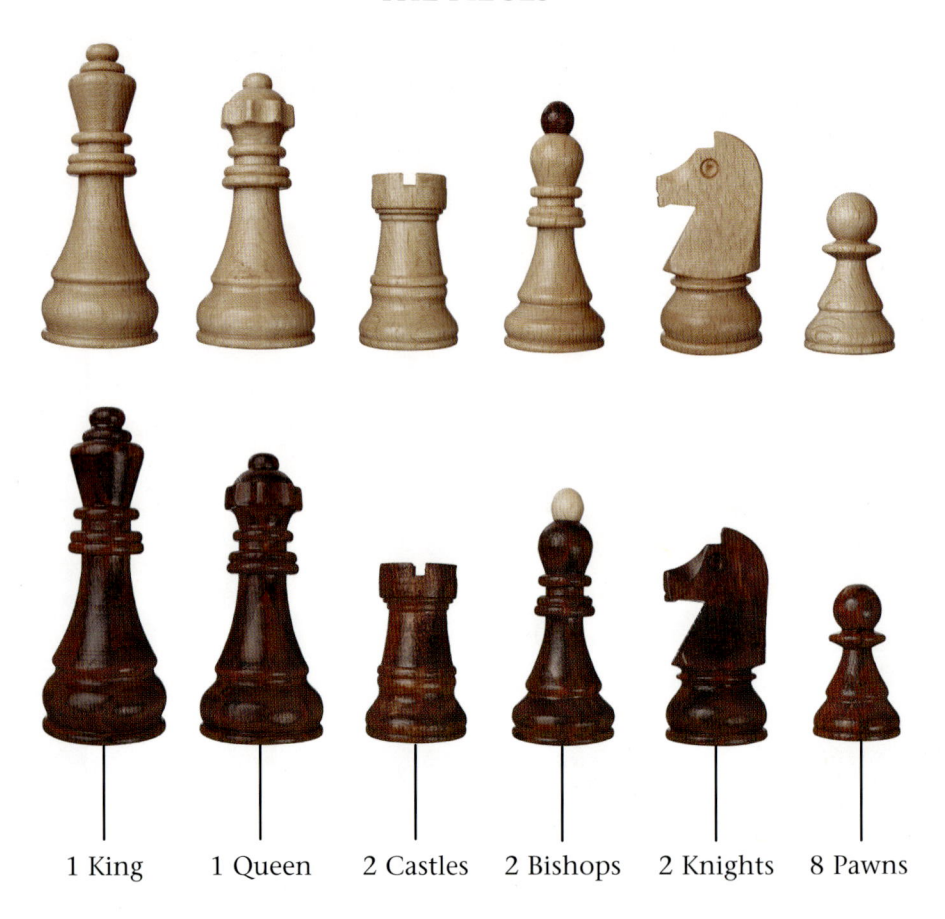

1 King   1 Queen   2 Castles   2 Bishops   2 Knights   8 Pawns

WHERE DID CHESS COME FROM?

Most people think that the first type of chess was played in India in the 6th century. This game was called *chaturanga*, and it was the first game that was played using a board with squares and pieces that you move.

From India, the game was taken to Persia (now Iran), to Russia and then to Europe in the 11th century. In Europe, the pieces were changed to the ones we use now: King, Queen, Castles, Knights, Bishops and Pawns. By the 15th century, the rules of chess that we use today were set out.

About the author – Lewis Carroll

Lewis Carroll's real name was Charles Lutwidge Dodgson. He was born in Cheshire, England, in 1832, and he was the oldest boy in a family of eleven children. As a child, he enjoyed making up games and he was very good at maths. When he was twenty years old, he went to study maths at Oxford University and he later became a lecturer.

He knew a little girl called Alice Liddell, and often told stories to her and her sisters. One day they all went on a picnic and he told them the story that became *Alice's Adventures in Wonderland*. When they arrived home, Alice asked him to write the story down and he did. It was published by Macmillan in 1865. He later wrote a second book about Alice called *Through the Looking-glass, and What Alice Found There*. There are Macmillan English Explorers versions of both of these books.

Lewis Carroll was also a very good photographer. He took pictures of famous people such as the poet Alfred Lord Tennyson, as well as the children he knew.

When he died in 1898, *Alice's Adventures in Wonderland* was the most popular children's book in England. This version of *Through the Looking-glass* contains the original artwork from when it was first published in 1872.